BUSINESS PLANS MADE E-Z

MADE E-Z PRODUCTS, Inc.
Deerfield Beach, Florida / www.MadeE-Z.com

Business Plans Made E-Z™
© copyright 2000 Made E-Z Products, Inc.
Printed in the United States of America

MADE E-Z
PRODUCTS

384 South Military Trail
Deerfield Beach, FL 33442
Tel. 954-480-8933
Fax 954-480-8906

http://www.MadeE-Z.com

1 2 3 4 5 6 7 8 9 10   CPC   R 10 9 8 7 6 5 4 3 2 1

Business Plans Made E-Z™

ISBN 1-56382-2

Table of contents

Introduction to Business Plans Made E-Z™

As the number of new businesses increased at an unbelievable rate in the late 1970s, the number of business failures increased at an even greater rate. Moving into the new millennium, 80% of new business start-ups now fail. Because of this growth cycle, the *Business Plan* became the necessary tool for managing business finances and growth.

The business plan has since become a standard means of forecasting, tracking and adjusting operations. In effect the complete "road map" of the company, its importance in business financing takes on a whole new meaning. Now, as we look at a comprehensive business plan, we see all company data can be useful.

A properly prepared business plan presents an entire synopsis of a given company: where it has come from, what it is presently accomplishing, and where it is likely headed in the future.

Regardless of your type of business—planning to expand, correcting a losing trend, or launching a new business—a complete and well-prepared business plan will help you become successful.

Preparing a complete business plan is more than an overnight task. It is the smartest tool you can use to ensure the success of your business.

Although there is no iron-clad technique for preparing a business plan, this guide leads you through the various reports and analyses you will have to prepare for your comprehensive business plan—all the necessary steps on the road to success.

Please note, according to generally accepted accounting procedures, the balance sheet always appears first in any listing of financial statements. Business Plans Made E-Z has taken this into account by arranging this presentation in a simple order of preparation which you will readily understand and help you complete your Business Plan successfully.

What is a business plan?

1

Chapter 1

What is a business plan?

What you'll find in this chapter:

- ➧ The importance of a business plan
- ➧ Why you need a business plan
- ➧ The components of a business plan
- ➧ Projecting the right image

A road map of your business

If you are starting a new business, you may be more concerned with your product, or choosing your company logo, than with exactly how you plan to succeed. While these are important, one of the first things you must do is create a solid, complete, and comprehensive business plan. Simply put, a business plan is a complete overview of your business—a collection of information about your company—everything from philosophies to finances.

For the fledgling business, a business plan is a crucial component of the start-up process, as it not only provides a framework from which you build and develop your company, but also allows prospective investors and lenders to see why they should finance your business in the first place, without having to bear the cost of a complete audit. You have made a statement that you not only know what you want your business to do, but you also know how to do it.

A business plan is just as crucial for the existing business wishing to expand. All too often, a business grows more rapidly than its internally generated cash can support. When profits are not large enough to carry the forecasted growth, the business' growth must slow and allow internal cash to "catch up" and keep pace with the expansion or it will be forced to borrow working capital to stay alive. In either situation, a solid and comprehensive business plan is an essential business tool.

A clearly conceived, well documented business plan that establishes goals and includes the use of *pro forma* statements and budgets to ensure financial control, helps establish your credibility—you know what you want to do, and that you know how to accomplish it.

To be successful, you must understand and use financial planning in your business. Eight of ten new businesses fail—primarily because of the lack of sound financial planning.

What is a business plan?

A *business plan* is a complete map of your equipment, products, finances, philosophies, commitments, and advertising and marketing data—a map which will prove to be the most valuable tool you can use to ensure the success of your business. It will also enable any prospective investor or lender to immediately and accurately evaluate your business and forecast its future.

If you use your business plan to arrange any type of financing it must explain, in great depth, what you plan to do with the borrowed money, and your plans to repay the debt.

Your business plan includes the sources of your business income and how it is used, a complete set of past and present financial statements, detailed budgets with projected outlooks and future directions, cash-flow analysis, income tax records and other supporting documentation.

For the remainder of this guide, assume that you are a small-business person, whose primary purpose in creating a business plan is to obtain financing—either for expansion or start-up.

Before you create your "road map to success" you must carefully analyze:

- how much your business wants to borrow

- the term of the loan

- how your business will repay the loan

- your back-up plan

- security and/or collateral you can offer the lender

Why you need a business plan

Financiers, money-lenders, and investors always look to place their money where it will bring them the greatest return. They look at a company's business plan as a quick reference guide to what the business has done in the past and where it is going in the future.

Careful screening of your company's business plan quickly discloses to the lender the data and trends of your business, and whether dollars should be risked with you and your company. The comprehensive business plan also indicates when a company—seemingly in financial peril—could be a sound investment. If that is your particular circumstance, then your business plan must also convey that message.

With the creation of your business plan you immediately climb up a rung on the ladder. You are no longer just another entrepreneur—you have a business plan!

Some dramatic lessons can be learned from those companies that, for one reason or another, failed to develop a business plan—or worse—did not follow the plan, once developed. For example:

> *Laker International Airlines, poised to become a multi-billion dollar business as Sir Freddie Laker's SkyTrain, charged the lowest fares between New York and London. Unfortunately, when not making mental notes, Sir Freddie wrote his business plans on odd scraps of paper, and failed to alert his business managers of the company's direction. Finally, in the mid-80's Laker International Airlines went bankrupt.*

Projecting the right image

Make your first impression a lasting one. Initially the prospective lender or investor will read your business plan for five minutes only. It must create a favorable impression on the lender during that first reading. Make sure every "i" is dotted, every "t" crossed, that no detail is omitted, and no figure forced. A wise lender can immediately pick out forced numbers—that is why he or she is a wise lender and you are looking at this person or institution to invest in your business.

Your business plan will be best received when you present it on high-quality stationery. Avoid patterned or "designer" papers. These actually tend to distract the reader and present a garish image opposed to the polished and professional look you want to present. Limit your paper choices to an eggshell or slightly off-white shade.

Type has proven easiest read in a serif font, such as *Times* at 12 point size. If you do not have a computer with a good word processing program and a quality printer, then have your business plan professionally typeset and printed. This is a very small price to pay for the results you expect to achieve.

Present the final product in a clear plastic binder or if large enough, even spiral bound. This can be accomplished quite reasonably at most office supply or copy stores.

Introducing your business plan

2

Chapter 2

Introducing your business plan

What you'll find in this chapter:

➡ The Cover Letter
➡ The Cover Sheet
➡ The Executive Summary
➡ The Table of Contents

Cover letter

While it is not included in your bound and completed business plan, attach a cover letter to your business plan, explaining what this package of papers is all about. Type the cover letter on your business stationery and briefly summarize:

- what you are looking for

- how it will be used

- what you are contributing

- how you will repay the debt

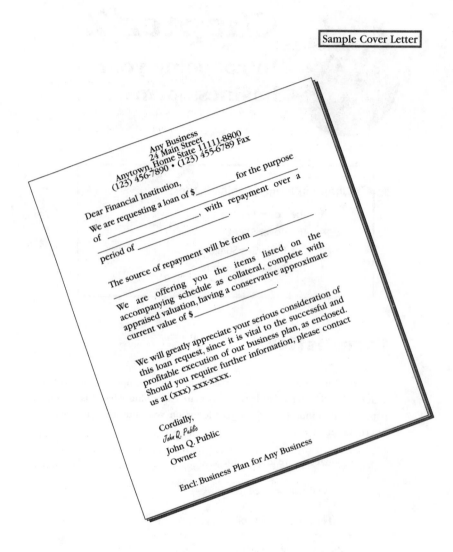

Any Business
24 Main Street
Anytown, Home State 11111-8800
(123) 456-7890 • (123) 455-6789 Fax

Dear Financial Institution,

We are requesting a loan of $_____ for the purpose
of _____, with repayment over a
period of _____.

The source of repayment will be from _____.

We are offering you the items listed on the
accompanying schedule as collateral, complete with
appraised valuation, having a conservative approximate
current value of $_____.

We will greatly appreciate your serious consideration of
this loan request, since it is vital to the successful and
profitable execution of our business plan, as enclosed.
Should you require further information, please contact
us at (xxx) xxx-xxxx.

Cordially,
John Q. Public
John Q. Public
Owner

Encl: Business Plan for Any Business

Cover sheet

The cover sheet (not a blank) is the first page of your business plan. It contains the name of your business, the address, telephone number(s), and lists the key contact people by name, address and phone number. By keeping this page clean and simple, the lender does not need to sift through the entire plan to find your contact information, and it keeps your business name in view.

Executive Summary

Your Executive Summary is the overall view of the business. It includes what you plan to do with the business, what it is capable of doing, how you intend to do it, who is responsible for meeting these goals, and how this will be financed. The Executive Summary is vital because financial investors and money-lenders often skim through most of the business plan, checking some figures along the way, but they *always* read the Executive Summary.

The entire summary should take up a single page with one paragraph per topic.

Table of Contents

The Table of Contents allows the lender to immediately pinpoint his/her principal area of interest, without having to read the entire document to find specific information. List each subject separately in the Table of Contents listing—even if that section is only one paragraph long.

Sample Cover Page

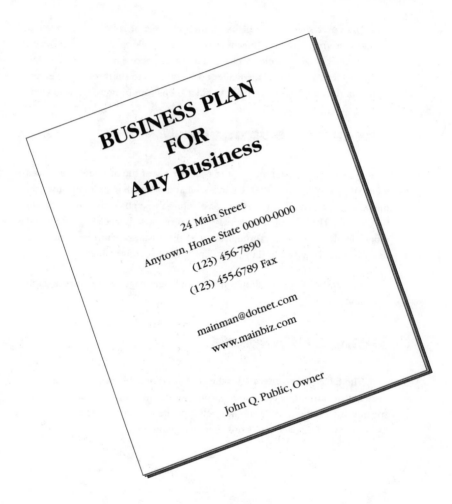

BUSINESS PLAN
FOR
Any Business

24 Main Street
Anytown, Home State 00000-0000
(123) 456-7890
(123) 455-6789 Fax

mainman@dotnet.com
www.mainbiz.com

John Q. Public, Owner

Sample Executive Summary

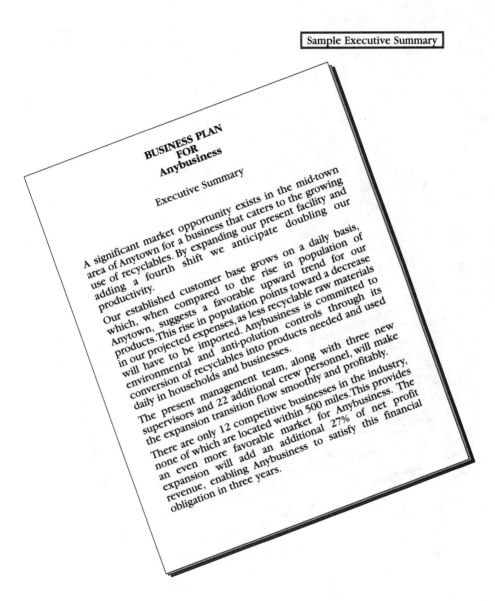

BUSINESS PLAN
FOR
Anybusiness

Executive Summary

A significant market opportunity exists in the mid-town area of Anytown for a business that caters to the growing use of recyclables. By expanding our present facility and adding a fourth shift we anticipate doubling our productivity.

Our established customer base grows on a daily basis, which, when compared to the rise in population of Anytown, suggests a favorable upward trend for our products. This rise in population points toward a decrease in our projected expenses, as less recyclable raw materials will have to be imported. Anybusiness is committed to its environmental and anti-polution controls through its conversion of recyclables into products needed and used daily in households and businesses.

The present management team, along with three new supervisors and 22 additional crew personnel, will make the expansion transition flow smoothly and profitably. There are only 12 competitive businesses in the industry, none of which are located within 500 miles. This provides an even more favorable market for Anybusiness. The expansion will add an additional 27% of net profit revenue, enabling Anybusiness to satisfy this financial obligation in three years.

BUSINESS PLAN FOR
Any Business
Table of Contents

Identifying your business

3

Chapter 3

Identifying your business

In this section of your business plan you carefully and methodically begin to map your entire business. You now list all of the details that clearly identify and distinguish your business from all others.

1) Identity of your business

- the business name and/or dba (doing business as)

- business mailing address

- physical address (if different)

- telephone number(s) and fax number

- tax and/or business registration numbers

- the purpose of your business as stated in the Articles of Incorporation or similar statement

- executives and contact addresses

- accountant of record and contact information

- attorney of record and contact information

- banker of record and contact information

- insurance agent of record and contact information

- other business consultants and their contact information

2) Your statement of purpose

Also known as a *Mission Statement*, this should be realistic enough to accurately describe your intentions yet appear optimistic. Begin with the nature and purpose of your business and a brief history of the company. Then move on to company products and/or services and your plans for expansion and growth. Finally, discuss how these plans will be put into effect. The Mission Statement runs a very close parallel to the Executive Summary you have just prepared.

Your statement of purpose includes:

- nature and purpose of the company

    Sample clause: *XYZ. Corp. was incorporated as a "C" corporation, under the laws of the state of Florida in 1990, for the purpose of manufacturing furniture from recycled materials.*

- history of the company's development

    Sample clause: *As stockpiles of recyclables began to accumulate, XYZ Corp. realized this abundance of*

*"raw" materials could be processed and molded. XYZ
Corp. developed the molds from which most of its
furniture components are made.*

- nature of the product and/or service

  Sample clause: *XYZ Corp. is able to replicate almost
  any furniture traditionally fabricated from wood and
  wood products. Because of the high-density achieved
  from blended materials, XYZ furniture is lighter in
  weight, and more durable than wood products.*

- manner in which the product and/or service will be created

  Sample clause: *XYZ manufactures its products through
  the "melting and blending" of the raw materials, which
  are then poured into pre-cast molds, and finished in
  customers' preferred colors.*

3) Your personnel

List your management and key personnel, the nature of their jobs, and
the role they will play in your plans for growth or expansion. Then, do the
same for your key technical and professional employees. The more staff
expertise you show, the more important your whole program becomes.

  Sample clause: *The management structure of XYZ
  Corp. shall consist of a Board of Directors, comprised of
  the president, vice-president, treasurer, and secretary,
  who have each been selected for their proven abilities
  to guide our company. The board of directors in turn
  will hire a business manager with a proven track
  record in our industry, to lead, develop, oversee and
  direct the daily operations of the company. The
  business manager will hire capable department
  managers, who will hire the skilled employees.*

PROFESSIONAL and TECHNICAL Sample:

Name: John Q. Doe
Address: 15 Someplace Lane, Anytown, USA
Phone/Fax: (000) 555-1212
E-mail: someone@somesite.net
Job Title: Analytical Chemist
Start Date: August 3, 1997
Salary: $1,000 per week
Work History: Imperial Chemical Industries
Senior Lab Supervisor, 4/12/85 to 7/31/97
Komex Chemical, Assistant Lab Supervisor,
7/14/75 to 3/31/85

4) Analysis of your product market

Briefly analyze the market for your product. Include these topics:

- Geographic market

  Sample clause: *XYZ Corp. realized its greatest success in urban areas, where customers are plentiful and material supply seemingly endless.*

- Market potential

  Sample clause: *Our product's potential market grows proportionately to the expansion of metropolitan areas. We also seek to serve these markets by introducing new furniture designs and products. It is estimated that by 2010 the estimated worldwide market will reach 300 million dollars.*

- Customers

  Sample clause: *XYZ Corp. enjoys strong customer support from young couples with and without children who demand greater value for their money.*

- Commercial customers

  Sample clause: *We have strong commercial roots in the non-professional sector of the business world where durability is more important than beauty.*

- Competition

  Sample clause: *Three other companies manufacture similar products.*

- Advantage over competitors

  Sample clause: *Since XYZ Corp. pioneered this concept of "recycled furniture," our name became the industry benchmark. XYZ Corp. has the shortest production cycle in the industry and thus, is first to market with new products.*

- Sales forecast

  Sample clause: *While XYZ Corp. anticipates a slight drop in new commercial customers, the boom in births over the past three years promises a banner non-commercial sales year.*

- Sales and distribution plan

  Sample clause: *To establish a number of regional warehouse outlets where customers may order and pick up our products.*

5) Production summary

Carefully present your production schedule and requirements, including such important items as:

- your production facilities

  Sample clause: *XYZ Corp. currently produces all products within a single 18,000 square foot warehouse. After pouring, the molds are cured in a separate 10,000 square foot storage building.*

- equipment used in production

    Sample clause: *Two smelters for melting the raw materials, six forklifts for transporting the molds and products, five delivery vehicles, and a full compliment of hand and power tools.*

- labor requirements

    Sample clause: *Currently, 57 skilled laborers complete our production staff. Anticipating a 200 percent increase in production requirements, we estimate hiring an additional 35 skilled and five managerial employees.*

- materials and supplies

    Sample clause: *Raw materials are continually acquired from community recycling centers. As the population increases, recyclable waste also increases. Therefore we anticipate no shortage of materials and no substantial increase in cost per unit.*

- shipping and transportation required

    Sample clause: *As each new regional warehouse is completed, XYZ Corp. will utilize subcontractors to facilitate shipping, resulting in an overall savings per unit.*

- existing quality control

    Sample clause: *One unit in every 15 manufactured is carefully inspected for overall quality and stress tested for durability.*

- special work force programs

    Sample clause: *XYZ Corp. has already contracted to annually accept three trainees from Handicap Industries, Inc.*

6) Daily schedule

Describe in detail a typical business day. Provide enough detail to give the reader a sense of the daily workings of the company.

Sample clause:

> *Mornings—All managers meet to outline daily production quotas. Barges leave to pick up raw materials. Smelters are fired. Castings from the previous shift are pulled from the molds which are cleaned and reset for the next filling. Castings are transported to cooling racks, where they are stored by order number. Raw material is sorted, graded and transported to the smelters.*
>
> *Midday—Molds are filled from the smelters. Barges leave to obtain more raw materials. Castings are brought to quality control where they are examined for flaws. Those that pass move to the finishing area where color is applied by hand, and the finish is mechanically applied. Finished castings are moved to the drying room.*
>
> *Afternoon—Cool molds are moved to the holding area where they continue cooling. Inspected castings are packed and shipped per order. Invoices are generated. Barges return with raw materials which are again sorted and graded. Barges are serviced and prepared for the next day. Areas are cleaned and prepared for the morning shift. Managers submit their paperwork to the office.*

7) Location

Evaluate your business location(s), and discuss why your business will grow and prosper in its present location or why you must relocate. You should also include a brief description of competition in your area and why this will have no negative impact upon your product or business growth.

- description of location

  Sample clause: *Our physical location lies in the factory district along the river, five blocks west of Main Street and two blocks south of Blinder Avenue.*

- benefits of location

  Sample clause: *XYZ Corp. is easily accessible from all main traffic arteries with no heavy congestion in the surrounding area. Its position along the river facilitates easy delivery of raw materials by barge, thus avoiding additional trucking or rail costs.*

- competition analysis by location

  Sample clause: *XYZ Corp. enjoys no competition within a 250-mile radius of its production facility.*

8) Repayment plan

Remember, your ultimate goal in preparing this business plan is to obtain a loan or investment in your business. At this point, state how the loan will help your product or business, how you plan to repay the borrowed money, and the repayment terms.

Your
financial
records

4

Chapter 4

Your financial records

Financial statements record the performance of your business and allow you to diagnose its strengths and weaknesses. This area of the business plan is the most time consuming, since it must also be the most exacting. Preparing the financials is a highly-detailed matter of entering the required figures onto the pages of your business plan—in all the right spots. Be advised that this area receives great attention from the prospective lender, so proceed carefully and diligently.

In this section you must make sure "A" plus "B" always equals "C," or that "C" minus "B" always equals "A." Most of your financial data will appear in the business plan a number of times, or be reflected somewhere else in the plan. Beware of "fudging the figures." You will fail to obtain the needed funds should you do so.

Source and use of funds

If you are already set up in business, your financials begin with a listing of current sources and uses of funds. This is an in-depth review of where all the money (income) comes from and how you have spent that money in the course of your business.

On the *Source and Use of Funds* form, list all of the sources and amounts of business income, including proceeds from mortgages, notes and loans payable to the business. The sum of these sources is **Total Income ❶**.

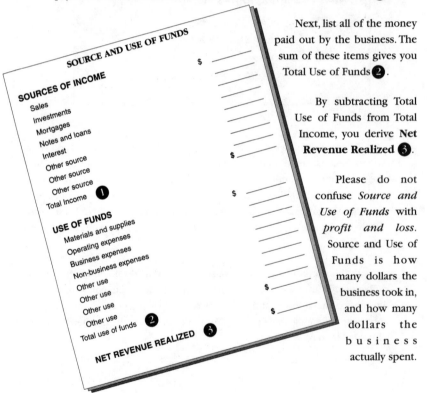

Next, list all of the money paid out by the business. The sum of these items gives you Total Use of Funds **❷**.

By subtracting Total Use of Funds from Total Income, you derive **Net Revenue Realized ❸**.

Please do not confuse *Source and Use of Funds* with *profit and loss*. Source and Use of Funds is how many dollars the business took in, and how many dollars the business actually spent.

Start-up capital

If you have not yet established yourself in business, or your purpose is to expand your business, you must prepare a statement of *Estimated Start-up Capital*. Here, you list how much you anticipate it is going to cost to start-up (or expand, or re-organize) your business. Your start-up capital schedule includes the one-time expenses (costs) required for growth or expansion.

On this form you list all the regular monthly business expenses you estimate will have to be paid until the start-up or expansion is complete and the business can take charge of its expenses again.

Modestly underestimating your business costs and expenses could be just as devastating as overestimating and being turned down. A number below what is needed to keep things running will cut your business short and put you right back into the money-hunt game.

ESTIMATED START-UP CAPITAL		
	Monthly Expenses	Cash Needed to Start
MONTHLY COSTS		
Salary of owners	$ _____	$ _____
Other salaries and wages	$ _____	$ _____
Rents	$ _____	$ _____
Advertising	$ _____	$ _____
Delivery expense	$ _____	$ _____
Supplies	$ _____	$ _____
Telephone	$ _____	$ _____
Utilities	$ _____	$ _____
Insurance	$ _____	$ _____
Taxes, including payroll taxes	$ _____	$ _____
Interest	$ _____	$ _____
Maintenance	$ _____	$ _____
Legal and professional fees	$ _____	$ _____
Miscellaneous expenses	$ _____	$ _____
Subtotal	$ _____	$ _____
ONE-TIME COSTS		
Equipment	$ _____	$ _____
Furniture and fixtures	$ _____	$ _____
Remodeling and decorating	$ _____	$ _____
Installation charges	$ _____	$ _____
Start-up inventory	$ _____	$ _____
Public utility deposits	$ _____	$ _____
Legal and professional fees	$ _____	$ _____
Licenses and permits	$ _____	$ _____
Advertising, promotion for opening	$ _____	$ _____
Petty cash	$ _____	$ _____
Other expenses	$ _____	$ _____
Subtotal	$ _____	$ _____
TOTAL ESTIMATED START-UP CAPITAL	$ _____	$ _____

Capital or long-term assets

Next, prepare a *Schedule of Capital Assets and Depreciation* (see sample on page 41) which includes items owned and those items subject to term payments (mortgages, etc.) such as:

● Buildings—Any permanent structure your business owns or plans to own as part of the growth process.

● Leasehold improvements—Permanent improvements (other than incidental repairs) which have been or will be made to any property you lease.

● Machinery and equipment—All machinery and equipment (other than furniture and fixtures) that have a useful life expectancy of more than one year.

● Furniture and fixtures—Furniture and other fixtures which you utilize in the execution of your business, but not in its production (i.e. desks, chairs, business computers, etc.).

● Vehicles—Cars, trucks, buses, etc.

● Signage—Permanently fixed items used to identify your business or product to the public may be considered a capital asset if you own the building, or if it is a "trade asset."

All of these capital (or long-term) assets are subject to depreciation (decrease in value over time), based on their **Useful Life Expectancy ❻**,which may be calculated by years or in percentages. In other words, if an asset is expected to last for five years, you would be entitled to deduct 20 percent of the cost of the asset as depreciation in each of the five years. After depreciation (both current and accumulated) is deducted from the cost, a net value remains.

Sample Schedule of Capital Assets

SCHEDULE OF CAPITAL ASSETS AND DEPRECIATION

① Item, Serial Number, or Description	② Date Acquired	③ Cost or Value	④ Recapture Value	⑤ Prior Depreciation Allowed or Allowable	⑥ Useful Life Expectancy	⑦ Paid in Full Yes / NO	⑧ Current Depreciation	⑨ Net Value Remaining
	/ /	$	$	$	Yrs. %	○ ○	$	$
	/ /	$	$	$	Yrs. %	○ ○	$	$
	/ /	$	$	$	Yrs. %	○ ○	$	$
	/ /	$	$	$	Yrs. %	○ ○	$	$
	/ /	$	$	$	Yrs. %	○ ○	$	$
	/ /	$	$	$	Yrs. %	○ ○	$	$
	/ /	$	$	$	Yrs. %	○ ○	$	$
	/ /	$	$	$	Yrs. %	○ ○	$	$
	/ /	$	$	$	Yrs. %	○ ○	$	$
	/ /	$	$	$	Yrs. %	○ ○	$	$
	/ /	$	$	$	Yrs. %	○ ○	$	$
	/ /	$	$	$	Yrs. %	○ ○	$	$
			TOTALS	$	⑩	⑪	$	
		Add Current Depreciation		$				
		Total Depreciation		$	⑫			

Net Value of Capital Assets $ ⑬

❷ **Date acquired** immediately shows if asset was acquired prior to—or during—the current accounting period. This is important because you can only claim depreciation for the amount of time you have owned the asset.

> *For example:* You purchased a tool in September. You cannot deduct depreciation for the entire year (based upon the item's *useful life expectancy*) because you have only owned it for four months. Now you must calculate depreciation as normal, but you may only deduct ⅓ (or 33⅓% of the full year's amount (or the 4 months of ownership).

❸ The **Cost or Value** of an asset is the dollar amount actually paid for the asset, or its fair market value if the asset was not acquired at retail.

❹ The **Recapture Value** of an asset (sometimes referred to as salvage value) is that amount which can still be realized from the sale of an asset after it has passed its life expectancy or usefulness—or becomes unrepairable. The recapture value cannot be depreciated.

For example: You have purchased a tool for $1000, and estimate its useful life expectancy to be three years and still have a recapture value of $37. By deducting the $37 recapture value from the cost, you arrive at a depreciable value of $963. For the purpose of this example, assume the tool was purchased on April 1, 1999 and you are preparing the *Schedule of Capital Assets and Depreciation* in 2000.

Depreciable value   = $963.00
÷ 3 years   = $321.00 annual depreciation
÷ 12 months   = $26.75 monthly depreciation
x 9 months of ownership = $240.27 current depreciation allowable

5 **Prior Depreciation Allowed or Allowable** is the total of all depreciation previously deducted.

6 **Useful Life Expectancy** is the number of years the asset is expected to endure until retirement. This may be calculated in years or converted to percentages, for example: four years useful life expectancy would convert to 25% allowable annual depreciation

6 **Paid in Full** is a helpful check-off to quickly see if an assets is debt-free.

8 **Current Depreciation** is calculated by dividing the Cost or Value less Recapture Value by the Useful Life Expectancy (or by multiplying the Cost or Value less the Recapture amount by the percentage rate).

Current Depreciation = (Cost or Value) - (Recapture Value) ÷ (Years of Useful Life Expectancy)
    or
Current Depreciation = (Cost or Value) - (Recapture Value) x (% of Useful Life Expectancy)

Preparing the *Schedule of Capital Assets and Depreciation* provides an additional benefit—you have also prepared a *Depreciation Schedule*—which you later need for your *Balance Sheet* and *Income Statement*.

By subtracting both **Prior** and **Current Depreciation** from **Cost or Value** you find the **Net Value Remaining** **9**.

(Net Value Remaining) = (Cost or Value) – (Prior + Current Depreciation)

To calculate **Total Depreciation 12** (needed on the Income Statement) add **Total Current Depreciation 11** and **Total Prior Depreciation 10** .

(Total Depreciation) = (Total Current Depreciation) + (Total Prior Depreciation.)

Add all of the **Net Value Remaining** figures to determine the **Net Value of All Capital Assets 13**, needed for the *Balance Sheet*.

Income Statements

Chapter 5

Income Statements

What you'll find in this chapter:

➡ Returns and allowances
➡ Listing inventories in cost of goods sold
➡ Calculating gross profit
➡ Operating expenses
➡ Finding net income or (loss)

While the balance sheet discussed in Chapter 6 reflects the basic financial position of your company at a specified point in time, the **Income Statement** (also known as a *Profit and Loss Statement*) details the flow of finances into and out of your business—over a specific period of time. The careful examination and comparison of income statements of several accounting periods will usually reveal where the business will go in the future.

The income statement shows the revenues from selling products and services and other income items, such as interest earned by your business. It also details all of the expenses incurred in the operation of your business. In addition, the income statement provides accountability for deducting depreciation and amortization (as discussed in Chapter 4), and income taxes which, while affecting the profitability of your company, may not be reflected in its cash flow.

The income statement lists and details:

1   **Gross income or revenue**—Where the business money came from and how much is received. This includes sales, interest received, and any other income (not necessarily listed in the sample on page 47) that is received during the course of business. This category also includes returns and allowances, which is deducted from income as products are returned or credit extended.

2   **Cost of goods sold**—This represents the cost of producing and selling your product and any other expense which is directly related to the manufacture or selling of your product or service—other than the actual operating expenses of your business.

To calculate Cost Of Goods Sold start with your inventory on hand at the beginning of a specific accounting period. Add your production and sales expenses to that amount. From their total deduct the inventory on the closing date of the accounting period to derive your cost of goods sold.

3   **Gross profit**—How much money is left after deducting the cost of goods sold from the business' income.

4   **Operating expenses**—Includes the remainder of business expenses which your business incurred, including: management, executive, and non-production payroll, rent, etc.. Here you account for depreciation and/or amortization and deduct them. The total operating expense is deducted from the gross profit.

Other income and other expenses—(Not shown in the sample on page 47.) These items would be listed for business income or business expenses *not directly related to* your normal course of business. Other income and other expenses are respectively added or deducted from the sub-total of gross profit less operating expenses.

Sample Income Statement

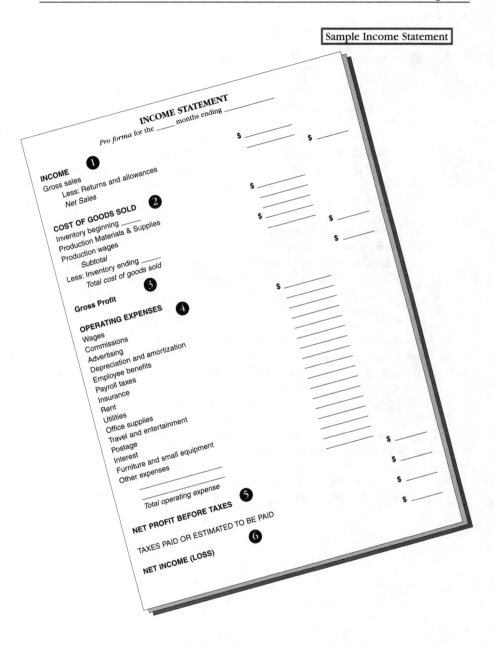

INCOME STATEMENT

Pro forma for the _____ months ending _____

$ _____ $ _____

INCOME ❶
Gross sales
  Less: Returns and allowances
  Net Sales

COST OF GOODS SOLD ❷
Inventory beginning _____
Production Materials & Supplies
Production wages
  Subtotal
Less: Inventory ending _____
  Total cost of goods sold

Gross Profit ❸

OPERATING EXPENSES ❹
Wages
Commissions
Advertising
Depreciation and amortization
Employee benefits
Payroll taxes
Insurance
Rent
Utilities
Office supplies
Travel and entertainment
Postage
Interest
Furniture and small equipment
Other expenses

Total operating expense

NET PROFIT BEFORE TAXES ❺

TAXES PAID OR ESTIMATED TO BE PAID ❻

NET INCOME (LOSS)

5 **Net profit before taxes**—The amount of profit which your business has generated in the course of operations is also known as the EIBT (earned income before taxes). This is the amount of income which is subject to state and federal taxation.

Income taxes—Deduct taxes which have been paid (or estimated to be paid) to state and federal governments here. If the taxes have already been paid, the account is labeled *Income taxes paid*. If the taxes have not been paid, Label the account *Allowance for income taxes*, or *Estimated income taxes to be paid*.

6 **Net profit (or loss)**—The bottom line! The amount of true profit (or loss) your business has made (or lost), after all expenses and taxes have been deducted. In accounting terms, anytime a (loss) or negative amount appears, it is designated by enclosing the number in brackets. This prevents the number from being misconstrued as anything other than a negative number.

The first income statement included in your business plan should be a *pro forma plan*, which is a representation (or projection) of what you anticipate the business' financial situation to be in the future. Although it is only a projection based on educated guesswork, it should still be as close as possible to the business' actual future financial position.

Note—In order to keep your business plan as up-to-date as possible, this will probably be one of the last items you complete.

For an existing business, you should also add income statements from each of the last three complete years you have been in business.

Balance sheets

Chapter 6

Balance sheets

What you'll find in this chapter:

▸ Tangible and intangible assets

▸ Accounting periods

▸ Pro formas

▸ Assets, liabilities, and net worth

The balance sheet provides an overall picture of the financial health of your business at any given moment, usually at the close of an accounting period. It lists in detail those tangible and intangible items the business owns (known as assets), and all money the business owes, either to its creditors (liabilities) or to its owners (shareholders' equity or net worth).

Tangible and intangible are two words which often confuse people. In very simple terms, *tangible* could be substituted with the word "real," or something that you can see and touch. *Intangible* refers to things which do have value, but do not exist to sight or touch, such as the value of goodwill.

An *accounting period* refers to a typically used and accepted time frame. An acceptable accounting period could be one week, one month, three months (or quarter), a half-year, or the full year. Another important term is the *fiscal year*. A fiscal year, simply put, is any accounting year which ends on a date other than December 31st.

Example: If you started your business on September 15, you could exercise the option of *always* ending your accounting year on September 14th, and filing all of your tax forms, etc. effective as of that date. However, once you make this election for fiscal year accounting, it would involve a tedious amount of paperwork to change it back to a calendar year accounting period. Plan this out well before making any final decision.

Balance sheets show exactly what their name states—the balance point of your business. They indicate to the prospective lender the amount of the business' assets, liabilities, and equity or net worth. The balance sheet formula must always be kept in balance, i.e. "assets = liabilities + net worth."

Pro forma

The first balance sheet included in your business plan should be *pro forma*—a projection. The pro forma balance sheet is a hypothetical balance sheet based on a set of assumptions—how you anticipate you business to look on a specific date.

Note—In order to keep your business plan as up-to-date as possible, this will probably be one of the last items you complete.

Assets

Assets are items which represent dollars invested. Assets include not only cash, merchandise inventory, land, machinery and equipment, and intellectual property (patents, trademarks and copyrights), but also money due the business from individuals or businesses (known as receivables).

Receivables are amounts of money or credit due the business. If you sell your product or services with no immediate cash received, or if payment is due over a specified time, you would have "accounts receivable," or money that is owed to your business. If your business has lent money or products to others you would then have products, loans, notes, or mortgages receivable. Unless the receivables are scheduled to be collected over a long period of time, they would be included in *liquid* or *short-term assets*.

Arrange assets in decreasing order of how quickly they can be turned into cash (liquidity).

- *Short-term (liquid) assets* are items that are convertible to immediate cash or readily convertible within a short period of time, generally considered in terms of one year or less, i.e. cash-on-hand or in banks, securities, bonds, inventories, pre-paid expenses, short-term receivables and certificates of deposit.

- *Capital* or *long-term assets* are identical to the capital asset list you completed in the last chapter. Capital assets are normally not held for resale, and are recorded on the balance sheet at their net value. Capital assets are subject to depreciation or amortization (a deduction for wear, tear or usage and depletion—in the case of resources such as an ore mine) and depreciation or amortization must be deducted from the original value to arrive at a true current or market value (refer to sample on page 41).

- Other assets include intangible assets (often referred to as *Intellectual Assets*), such as royalties, royalty arrangements, copyrights, patents, exclusive use contracts, and notes receivable from officers and employees.

Liabilities

Liabilities are amounts that you owe to others. Liabilities may also be classified as short- or long-term. Liabilities are listed in the order of how soon they must be repaid.

- *Short-term liabilities* generally include amounts payable to others, due in one year or less. These could be accounts payable on equipment, products or merchandise purchased, sight drafts, credit card payments, etc. This classification should also include the current portion of any long-term liabilities.

- *Long-term liabilities* include notes, loans, bonds or mortgages, which have a payback term greater than one year.

Capital

Capital or net worth represents the true dollar value of your business. Net worth is the assets of the business minus its liabilities, and it equals the *owners' (or stockholders') equity*. This equity is the investment made by the owner or stockholders (if your business is incorporated) plus any profits or minus any losses that have accumulated in the business. Items in the net worth category include:

- *Owners' (or stockholders') equity*—The current value of what the owners (or stockholders) have contributed to the business thus far.

- *Retained earnings*—Funds that have not been distributed or spent as yet (including the profits from the current period).

The combination of owners' equity and retained earnings (profit from this period) is called the equity, net worth, or capital of a business. Of course, when dealing with large corporations, there are many other terms and classifications, including listings for paid-in capital stock, capital stock issued and outstanding, stock surplus, capital distributions, dividends, etc.

To prepare your balance sheet, you first list the short-term assets, and add them to show Total Short-term Assets **1**. Then list the long-term assets and add those amounts to show Total Long-term Assets **2**. Next you add any Intangible and/or Intellectual Assets (if any are owned), and this total is Total Intangible/Intellectual Assets, following in the same format as short- and long-term assets. The totals of those categories are then added together to show Total Assets. **3**

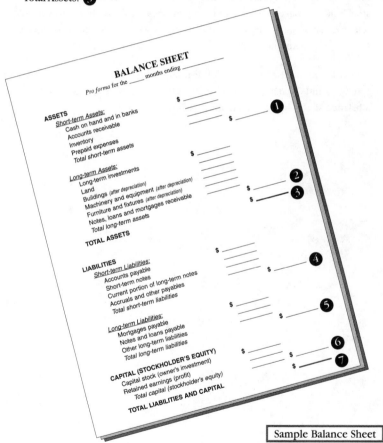

Sample Balance Sheet

Now follow the same procedure for liabilities. First list and total short-term liabilities ❹, then list and total long-term liabilities ❺. The sum of their totals is called Total Liabilities.

Capital and stockholders equity can sometimes be difficult to ascertain, but since you have followed good accounting practices up to this point, you will have no problems. First calculate the total of the amounts you (and/or the stockholders) have invested into the business. To that number you add the retained earnings or profits of the business for the period. This equals Total Capital (or stockholders' equity) ❻.

Add the total of Capital to the total of Liabilities and you arrive at Total Liabilities and Capital ❼, which **MUST EQUAL** Total Assets. This is why it is called a balance sheet—the numbers must balance.

Budgets and Analyses

7

Chapter 7

Budgets and Analysis

What you'll find in this chapter:

- ➠ Uses of a budget
- ➠ Components of a budget
- ➠ Break-even analysis
- ➠ Average selling price per unit
- ➠ Break-even point

Budgets

A *budget* is a very useful tool to help you map how much income you expect to receive and how much you plan to spend. When closely watched, a budget informs you if you are over- or under-pricing your product or service. It will also clearly indicate overruns in expenses.

Set realistic income and expense goals for the company's budget. If a budget is planned too tightly, then cutting costly corners and compromising the quality of the product could result.

The budgets should be prepared on a monthly and annual basis—as of a specific date and accounting period, and be divided into three sections:

Sample Monthly Budget

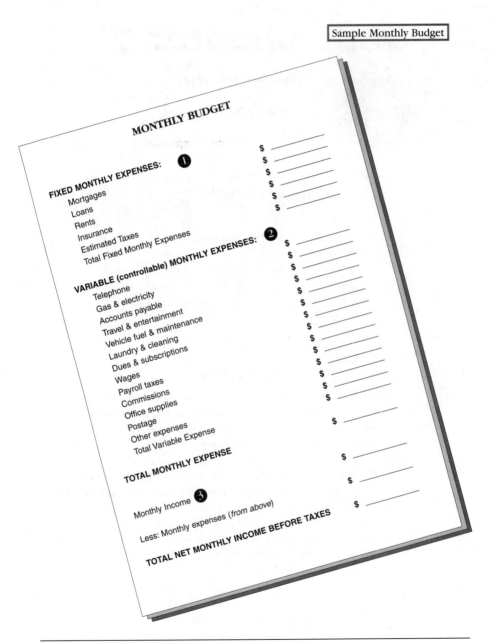

MONTHLY BUDGET

FIXED MONTHLY EXPENSES: ❶

Mortgages $ _____
Loans $ _____
Rents $ _____
Insurance $ _____
Estimated Taxes $ _____
Total Fixed Monthly Expenses $ _____

VARIABLE (controllable) MONTHLY EXPENSES: ❷

Telephone $ _____
Gas & electricity $ _____
Accounts payable $ _____
Travel & entertainment $ _____
Vehicle fuel & maintenance $ _____
Laundry & cleaning $ _____
Dues & subscriptions $ _____
Wages $ _____
Payroll taxes $ _____
Commissions $ _____
Office supplies $ _____
Postage $ _____
Other expenses $ _____
Total Variable Expense $ _____

TOTAL MONTHLY EXPENSE $ _____

Monthly Income ❸ $ _____

Less: Monthly expenses (from above) $ _____

TOTAL NET MONTHLY INCOME BEFORE TAXES

① **Fixed Monthly Expenses**—Are monthly expenses that seldom, if ever, vary regardless of the quantity of production. These include rent, mortgage, liens, insurance, and taxes. Items which are not going to fluctuate whether production is 250 items or 25,000, are considered fixed budget items.

② **Variable (controllable) Monthly Expenses**—Expenses which you are able to control through usage such as, but not limited to, telephone, utilities, wages, commissions, postage, laundry, and vehicle expenses. Do not classify raw materials and component parts as fixed expenses. While they may have a set value per unit, as the number of units produced fluctuates, so will the dollar value of the "raw materials." Therefore, raw material and component parts are a variable expense.

③ **Monthly Income**—The sources and amounts of revenue your business receives (or anticipates receiving) each month appears as a total dollar amount. This figure could be the same as Total Income on the Sources and Uses of Funds page, or you may increase or decrease this amount for your budget.

Break-even analysis

A *break-even analysis* is important, not only for your business plan, but also in your routine financial analysis. "Break-even" means the level of operations at which a business neither makes a profit nor incurs a loss. At the break-even point, income is just enough to cover expenses.

The break-even analysis enables you to study the relationship of volume, costs, and revenue. It also requires you to define the sales level—either in terms of income dollars or units sold within a given period—at which your business would earn zero profit and thus, break even.

A break-even analysis helps the prospective money-lender gauge the probable success or failure of business, and it is one tool which even a long-experienced business can fail to utilize properly. A wise business owner better controls his/her profit margin through an annual break-even analysis.

The well-prepared break-even analysis is composed of two parts—fixed costs and variable costs.

Your first step in calculating your break-even point is to carefully analyze the cost of the product. This can be done either on a *per unit* basis or on a *total units produced* basis. It is important to note that once you begin to calculate on either the per unit or total units basis, you must continue your calculations in that same format.

The *average cost of the product* ❶ consists of a fixed cost and a controllable cost. Both costs are listed separately. The fixed portion is that amount which is going to remain constant regardless of how many units are produced.

> **For example:** If the cost of a single widget used as a component in your product is $1.00 and assuming no increase in your raw cost, that amount is going to remain fixed at $1.00 whether you purchase 1 widget or 500 widgets.

Monthly selling expenses ❷ represents the amount you spend per month on advertising, sales salaries and commissions, or any other expenses directly tied to selling your product. *Monthly general expenses* ❸ represents the remainder of your normal expenses for the month.

Total all of the expenses for both fixed and controllable costs. ❹

From your other records you can easily obtain the *number of units produced* ❺ and *average selling price per unit* ❻. Insert those numbers in their respective positions.

Sample Break-even Analysis

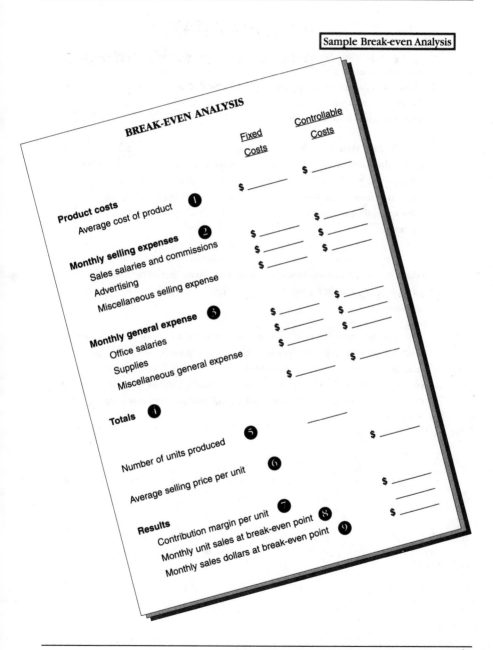

BREAK-EVEN ANALYSIS

	Fixed Costs	Controllable Costs
		$ _____
	$ _____	
Product costs ❶		
Average cost of product		$ _____
Monthly selling expenses ❷	$ _____	$ _____
Sales salaries and commissions	$ _____	$ _____
Advertising	$ _____	
Miscellaneous selling expense		
		$ _____
Monthly general expense ❸	$ _____	$ _____
Office salaries	$ _____	$ _____
Supplies	$ _____	
Miscellaneous general expense		$ _____
	$ _____	
Totals ❶	_____	
		$ _____
Number of units produced ❺		
Average selling price per unit ❻		$ _____
		_____
Results	Contribution margin per unit ❼ ❽	$ _____
Monthly unit sales at break-even point ❾		
Monthly sales dollars at break-even point		

To determine the *contribution margin per unit* ⑦ , first add the fixed and controllable costs. Then, divide their total by the number of units produced. This quotient represents the *average cost per unit*. Now subtract the average cost per unit from the average selling price per unit to find your contribution margin per unit.

To find your *monthly unit sales at break-even point* ⑧ , you must divide the total of your fixed and controllable costs by the average selling price per unit. This will effectively tell you how many units you must sell to reach the zero point. That is, no profit—no loss. If your average of monthly sales exceeds this number, then you are headed up the road to profit and success.

If they do not, you must immediately put on the brakes and begin an in-depth evaluation of your business. Either your costs are too high, or your sales are too low. In either case, you must formulate a strategy to correct this situation.

The last calculation in the results section is *monthly sales dollars at break-even point* ⑨ . Multiply the average selling price by the monthly unit sales at break-even point to find monthly sales dollars. If you have completed your math correctly, you can readily see that this is another form of balancing the records—as the monthly sales dollars and total product costs are the same number.

Cash-flow analysis

Chapter 8
Cash-flow analysis

What you'll find in this chapter:
- ⟹ Purpose of the cash-flow analysis
- ⟹ Relationship to the budget
- ⟹ Forcing fugures

Imagine you are preparing to purchase a home. Would you consider purchasing that home based solely on a photograph taken from the rooftop of a building across the street? Now compare this scenario to the viewpoint of a prospective lender. Just as you would not purchase that house on a view from the rooftop, the lender is not going to "purchase" your business based on one image.

Thus far, you have seen many forms that appear similar—yet they are not. Each form serves a different purpose in your financial plan and projects another view of your business to the prospective lender.

In Chapter 1, a strong warning was issued about "forcing figures," or just plugging in numbers to make one particular form look good. Now you can readily see why so many images are needed to present an accurate picture of your business. The prospective lender is examining whether the roof is laid on well supported beams, sitting on well-structured walls constructed on a rock-solid foundation.

The next step toward completing your successful business plan is the cash-flow analysis. Related to the *Source and Use of Funds* form, the cash-flow analysis shows the amount of actual cash that flows into and out of your business. It allows you (or a prospective lender) to determine whether income and expenses are more or less than the amount you had budgeted.

The cash-flow analysis begins with the balance of cash on hand at the beginning of the accounting period ❶ and adds cash from operations, which coincides with net revenue realized, as reported on the *Source and Use of Funds* form. This sum is labeled *Total Available Cash*. Deductions from total available cash include:

- **Operating expenses**—This includes cost of goods sold and operating expenses carried over from the income statement.

- **Capital expenditures**—These are payments made for the purchase of capital assets, but does not include interest or any other expenses deducted previously.

- **Interest and dividends**—This is interest paid on notes, loans and mortgages, and any dividends paid (under a corporate structure).

- **Debt retirement**—These are payments of principal on notes and investments.

After deducting these items from the total available cash, the balance is called *cash surplus* (or deficit) ❸. At this point any additional non-business revenues would be listed, such as notes and loans receivable or capital stock issued. The sum of any additions and cash surplus now equals the *closing cash balance*—which must correspond to *cash on hand and in banks* on the current Balance Sheet ❹.

Sample Cash-flow Analysis

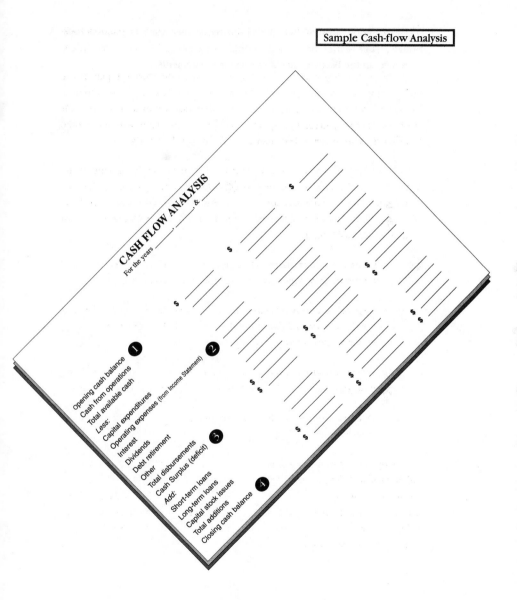

CASH FLOW ANALYSIS

For the years _____ & _____

Opening cash balance ❶
Cash from operations
Total available cash
Less:
Capital expenditures
Operating expenses (from Income Statement) ❷
Interest
Dividends
Debt retirement
Other
Total disbursements
Cash Surplus (deficit) ❸
Add:
Short-term loans
Long-term loans
Capital stock issues
Total additions
Closing cash balance ❹

A cash-flow analysis should be prepared in one-year and multiple year formats. The year(s) addressed should correspond to the same years referenced in the Balance Sheets and Income Statements.

Your marketing plan and other documents

9

Chapter 9

Your marketing plan and other documents

What you'll find in this chapter:

➠ Your market analysis

➠ Analyzing your product or service

➠ Marketing strategies and market mix

➠ Supporting documentation

Your marketing plan

You are now in the final stage of completing your successful business plan. In this segment you will finally have the chance to become creative and to demonstrate how much you know about your business (or the business you are planning to start-up).

Here you must effectively convince your prospective lender that your plan is a winner. Begin preparing your marketing plan by detailing your *Target Market*.

Market analysis

Target Market

Discuss what products, lines or services you will be offering and in what geographical areas you plan to sell them. Expand this by relating how you plan to introduce your product or service into this market, and how much money your target market will be willing to spend on *your* product or service.

Competition

Honestly evaluate your competition. Explain who they are and where they are physically located. Discuss how their product is different from yours, and how competitive they are in the market. Detail how long the competition has existed and their market penetration. Analyze similar products and/or services. Compare and contrast the products. List the disadvantages and advantages of your product.

Environment

Discuss the market environment of your product. Detail the important economic factors that affect your product or service. Explain any legal factors that may influence your product or service—noise, air pollution, or other environmental factors over which you have no control.

Product or service analysis

Description

Explain exactly what your product or service is. List what purposes it serves to benefit the user. Explain why the user would choose your product or service.

Comparison

Detail what advantages your product or service has over that of the competition. Consider such things as uniqueness, patents, expertise for use or special training. Explain if this presents any advantages or disadvantages. Discuss where materials for your product or service will come from, and any market influences your suppliers might create for you.

Market mix

Image

Discuss your product or service image. Provide a detailed explanation of how you wish your product or service to appear to the customers (cheap but good, exclusivity, or customer-oriented).

Features

List the features of your product or service that you are planning to emphasize, such as: greater cleaning power, more area coverage, new bio-degradable formula.

Pricing

Explain how your pricing strategy will help promote your product or service, in terms of:

- percentage of profit
- suggested selling price
- premium price
- competitive price

Customer services

If you intend to provide customer services, explain what they are. Discuss cash vs. credit terms, and how their use would affect your sales volume. Does the competition offer these services?

Advertising/Promotion

Discuss advertising and promotional tactics, the media you wish to use, and explain the message you will convey. Then explain the reasons you have chosen those media sources (circulation, cost effectiveness, market segmentation).

Other documents

The final pages of your successful business plan provide the supporting documentation that lends credibility to your business, your motivations, and your intentions.

The first documents which should appear in this section are the *federal and state tax returns,* including tangible personal property tax returns (if any are required by your state). The tax returns are of tremendous value to the lender in verifying the information you have provided.

Following the income tax returns, add *resumes of your key personnel.* These allow the lender to further determine if the business is in the hands of competent people.

Copies of current leases, loans, and mortgages inform the lender of obligations you are expected to fulfill or, in the case of income and receivables, of additional revenues you anticipate receiving.

Contracts, patents and trademarks (also known as intellectual assets) owned or in force, advise the lender about businesses you have already committed to, or have committed to you, as well as how much income you will receive from or have to spend on patent and/or trademark royalties.

Letters of reference give you and your business further credibility. These letters may be references from your suppliers about your purchase and payment practices, from trade associates regarding their business dealings with you, or from your bankers and/or other lenders, reinforcing your abilities to meet your present and future financial obligations.

By continually focusing on your business plan you are able to more clearly see and understand what your business is, how it operates, and what you can realistically expect in the future.

A
SAMPLE
BUSINESS
PLAN

Enlarging Forms Included in this Guide

1. Align center of form with mid-point on the glass plate guide—FACE DOWN.

2. Set the copy machine to print in the same format as the form is set on the glass—portrait or landscape.

3. Set the copy machine for enlargement to 122% of the original form.

4. Press the copy button.

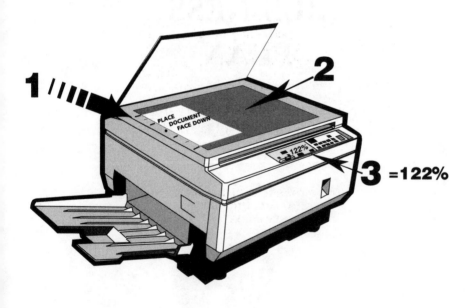

BUSINESS PLAN

FOR

BE SURE TO INCLUDE THE ABOVE
INFORMATION ON YOUR
COVER SHEET

BUSINESS PLAN FOR

_____

COVER LETTER

BUSINESS PLAN FOR

Table of Contents

IDENTIFYING INFORMATION

Name of Company: _____

DBA Name(s): _____

Address: _____

_____

Telephone(s): _____ Fax: _____

E-mail: _____ Web Site: _____

Description of Business: _____

_____

_____

Form of Business Entity: _____ Date Formed: _____

For a New Business:
The nature and purpose of the business shall be: _____

_____

_____

_____

For an Existing Business:
Length of Operation: _____

The nature of the expansion of the business is: _____

_____

_____

_____

eral Employer I.D. #: _____

e Employer I.D. #: _____

e/County Occupational License #: _____

cutive Name: _____ Phone: _____
ress: _____

cutive Name: _____ Phone: _____
ress: _____

cutive Name: _____ Phone: _____
ress: _____

cutive Name: _____ Phone: _____
ress: _____

cutive Name: _____ Phone: _____
ress: _____

ountant Name: _____ Phone: _____
ress: _____

rney Name: _____ Phone: _____
ress: _____

rney Name: _____ Phone: _____
ress: _____

ker Name: _____ Phone: _____
ress: _____

ker Name: _____ Phone: _____
ress: _____

rance Agent Name: _____ Phone: _____
ress: _____

rance Name: _____ Phone: _____
ress: _____

er Consultant Name: _____ Phone: _____
ress: _____

STATEMENT OF PURPOSE

The nature and purpose of this company is: _____

_____

_____

_____

_____

The history of this company's development is: _____

_____

_____

_____

The nature of the product and/or service shall be: _____

_____

_____

_____

The manner in which this product/service shall be created is: _____

_____

_____

_____

_____

MANAGEMENT AND KEY PERSONNEL

The members/directors/partners/managers of the business are:

Name: _____   Name: _____

Address: _____   Address: _____

_____   _____

Phone/Fax: _____   Phone/Fax: _____

E-mail: _____   E-mail: _____

Position: _____   Position: _____

Contributions to Business: _____ Contributions to Business: _____

_____   _____

Name: _____   Name: _____

Address: _____   Address: _____

_____   _____

Phone/Fax: _____   Phone/Fax: _____

E-mail: _____   E-mail: _____

Position: _____   Position: _____

Contributions to Business: _____ Contributions to Business: _____

_____   _____

Name: _____   Name: _____

Address: _____   Address: _____

_____   _____

Phone/Fax: _____   Phone/Fax: _____

E-mail: _____   E-mail: _____

Position: _____   Position: _____

Contributions to Business: _____ Contributions to Business: _____

_____   _____

The management structure of the business shall be: _____

_____

_____

_____

_____

_____

PROFESSIONAL AND TECHNICAL

Name: _____

Address: _____

_____

Phone/Fax: _____

E-mail: _____

Job Title: _____

Start Date: _____

Salary: _____

Work History: _____

_____

_____

Name: _____

Address: _____

_____

Phone/Fax: _____

E-mail: _____

Job Title: _____

Start Date: _____

Salary: _____

Work History: _____

_____

_____

Name: _____

Address: _____

_____

Phone/Fax: _____

E-mail: _____

Job Title: _____

Start Date: _____

Salary: _____

Work History: _____

_____

_____

Name: _____

Address: _____

_____

Phone/Fax: _____

E-mail: _____

Job Title: _____

Start Date: _____

Salary: _____

Work History: _____

_____

_____

Name: _____

Address: _____

_____

Phone/Fax: _____

E-mail: _____

Job Title: _____

Start Date: _____

Salary: _____

Work History: _____

_____

_____

Name: _____

Address: _____

_____

Phone/Fax: _____

E-mail: _____

Job Title: _____

Start Date: _____

Salary: _____

Work History: _____

_____

_____

Name: _____

Address: _____

_____

Phone/Fax: _____

E-mail: _____

Job Title: _____

Start Date: _____

Salary: _____

Work History: _____

_____

_____

Name: _____

Address: _____

_____

Phone/Fax: _____

E-mail: _____

Job Title: _____

Start Date: _____

Salary: _____

Work History: _____

_____

_____

Name: _____

Address: _____

_____

Phone/Fax: _____

E-mail: _____

Job Title: _____

Start Date: _____

Salary: _____

Work History: _____

_____

_____

Name: _____

Address: _____

_____

Phone/Fax: _____

E-mail: _____

Job Title: _____

Start Date: _____

Salary: _____

Work History: _____

_____

_____

MARKET ANALYSIS

Market Area: _____

_____

Market Potential: _____

_____

Consumer Customers: _____

_____

Commercial Customers: _____

_____

Competition: _____

_____

Advantage over competitors: _____

_____

Sales forecast by category: _____

_____

_____

Sales and distribution plan: _____

_____

_____

PRODUCTION SUMMARY

Description of Facilities: _____

_____

_____

Description of Equipment: _____

_____

_____

Labor Requirements: _____

_____

Supplies Requirements: _____

_____

Shipping/Transportation: _____

_____

Quality Control: _____

_____

Special Workforce Plans/programs: _____

_____

_____

DAILY OPERATIONS

Morning: _____

_____

_____

_____

_____

_____

_____

_____

Midday: _____

_____

_____

_____

Afternoon: _____

_____

_____

_____

_____

Evening: _____

_____

_____

_____

_____

LOCATION

Description of Location: _____

_____

_____

_____

_____

Benefits of Location: _____

_____

_____

_____

_____

Location Competition Analysis: _____

_____

_____

_____

_____

_____

_____

_____

_____

_____

REPAYMENT PLAN

In consideration for the amount of $ _____ which will be invested into our

business _____ in the form of _____

_____

_____

we offer _____

_____

_____

_____

_____

which will be repaid _____

_____

_____

_____

_____

_____

_____

_____

_____

ESTIMATED START-UP CAPITAL

	Monthly Expenses	Cash Needed to Start
MONTHLY COSTS		
Salary of owners	$ _____	$ _____
Other salaries and wages	$ _____	$ _____
Rents	$ _____	$ _____
Advertising	$ _____	$ _____
Delivery expense	$ _____	$ _____
Supplies	$ _____	$ _____
Telephone	$ _____	$ _____
Utilities	$ _____	$ _____
Insurance	$ _____	$ _____
Taxes, including payroll taxes	$ _____	$ _____
Interest	$ _____	$ _____
Maintenance	$ _____	$ _____
Legal and professional fees	$ _____	$ _____
Miscellaneous expenses	$ _____	$ _____
Subtotal	$ _____	$ _____
ONE-TIME COSTS		
Equipment	$ _____	$ _____
Furniture and fixtures	$ _____	$ _____
Remodeling and decorating	$ _____	$ _____
Installation charges	$ _____	$ _____
Start-up inventory	$ _____	$ _____
Public utility deposits	$ _____	$ _____
Legal and professional fees	$ _____	$ _____
Licenses and permits	$ _____	$ _____
Advertising, promotion for opening	$ _____	$ _____
Petty cash	$ _____	$ _____
Other expenses	$ _____	$ _____
Subtotal	$ _____	$ _____
TOTAL ESTIMATED START-UP CAPITAL	$ _____	$ _____

SOURCE AND USE OF FUNDS

SOURCES OF INCOME

Sales $ _____

Investments   _____

Mortgages   _____

Notes and loans   _____

Interest   _____

Other source   _____

Other source   _____

Other source   _____

Total Income $ _____

USE OF FUNDS

Materials and supplies $ _____

Operating expenses   _____

Business expenses   _____

Non-business expenses   _____

Other use   _____

Other use   _____

Other use   _____

Other use   _____

Total use of funds $ _____

NET REVENUE REALIZED $ _____

SCHEDULE OF CAPITAL ASSETS AND DEPRECIATION

Item, Serial Number, or Description	Date Acquired	Cost or Value	Recapture Value	Prior Depreciation Allowed or Allowable	Useful Life Expectancy	Paid in Full Yes / No	Current Depreciation	Net Value Remaining
	/ /	$	$	$	Yrs. ____ %	○ ○	$	$
	/ /	$	$	$	Yrs. ____ %	○ ○	$	$
	/ /	$	$	$	Yrs. ____ %	○ ○	$	$
	/ /	$	$	$	Yrs. ____ %	○ ○	$	$
	/ /	$	$	$	Yrs. ____ %	○ ○	$	$
	/ /	$	$	$	Yrs. ____ %	○ ○	$	$
	/ /	$	$	$	Yrs. ____ %	○ ○	$	$
	/ /	$	$	$	Yrs. ____ %	○ ○	$	$
	/ /	$	$	$	Yrs. ____ %	○ ○	$	$
	/ /	$	$	$	Yrs. ____ %	○ ○	$	$
	/ /	$	$	$	Yrs. ____ %	○ ○	$	$
	/ /	$	$	$	Yrs. ____ %	○ ○	$	$

TOTALS $

Add Current Depreciation $

Total Depreciation $

Net Value of Capital Assets $

BALANCE SHEET

Pro forma for the _____ months ending _____

ASSETS

Short-term Assets:
Cash on hand and in banks	$ _____	
Accounts receivable	_____	
Inventory	_____	
Prepaid expenses	_____	
Total short-term assets		$ _____

Long-term Assets:
Long-term investments	$ _____	
Land	_____	
Buildings *(after depreciation)*	_____	
Machinery and equipment *(after depreciation)*	_____	
Furniture and fixtures *(after depreciation)*	_____	
Notes, loans and mortgages receivable	_____	
Total long-term assets		$ _____

TOTAL ASSETS $ _____

LIABILITIES

Short-term Liabilities:
Accounts payable	$ _____	
Short-term notes	_____	
Current portion of long-term notes	_____	
Accruals and other payables	_____	
Total short-term liabilities		$ _____

Long-term Liabilities:
Mortgages payable	$ _____	
Notes and loans payable	_____	
Other long-term liabilities	_____	
Total long-term liabilities		$ _____

CAPITAL (STOCKHOLDER'S EQUITY)
Capital stock (owner's investment)	$ _____	
Retained earnings (profit)	_____	
Total capital (stockholder's equity)	_____	$ _____

TOTAL LIABILITIES AND CAPITAL $ _____

BALANCE SHEET

For the years ended _____, _____, & _____.

ASSETS

Short-term Assets:

Cash on hand and in banks	$ _____	$ _____	$ _____
Accounts receivable	_____	_____	_____
Ending Inventory _____	_____	_____	_____
Prepaid expenses	_____	_____	_____
Total short-term assets	$ _____	$ _____	$ _____

Fixed Assets:

Long-term investments	$ _____	$ _____	$ _____
Land	_____	_____	_____
Buildings *(after depreciation)*	_____	_____	_____
Machinery and equipment *(after depreciation)*	_____	_____	_____
Furniture and fixtures *(after depreciation)*	_____	_____	_____
Notes, loans and mortgages receivable	_____	_____	_____
Total long-term assets	$ _____	$ _____	$ _____
TOTAL ASSETS	$ _____	$ _____	$ _____

LIABILITIES

Short-term Liabilities:

Accounts payable	$ _____	$ _____	$ _____
Short-term notes	_____	_____	_____
Current portion of long-term notes	_____	_____	_____
Accruals and other payables	_____	_____	_____
Total short-trem liabilities	$ _____	$ _____	$ _____

Long-term Liabilities:

Mortgages payable	$ _____	$ _____	$ _____
Notes and loans payable	_____	_____	_____
Other long-term liabilities	_____	_____	_____
Total long-term liabilities	$ _____	$ _____	$ _____

CAPITAL (STOCKHOLDER'S EQUITY)

Capital stock (owner's investment)	$ _____	$ _____	$ _____
Retained earnings (profit)	_____	_____	_____
Total capital (stockholder's equity)	$ _____	$ _____	$ _____
TOTAL LIABILITIES AND CAPITAL	$ _____	$ _____	$ _____

MONTHLY BUDGET

FIXED MONTHLY EXPENSES:

Mortgages	$ _____
Loans	$ _____
Rents	$ _____
Insurance	$ _____
Estimated Taxes	$ _____
Total Fixed Monthly Expenses	$ _____

VARIABLE (controllable) MONTHLY EXPENSES:

Telephone	$ _____
Gas & electricity	$ _____
Accounts payable	$ _____
Travel & entertainment	$ _____
Vehicle fuel & maintenance	$ _____
Laundry & cleaning	$ _____
Dues & subscriptions	$ _____
Wages	$ _____
Payroll taxes	$ _____
Commissions	$ _____
Office supplies	$ _____
Postage	$ _____
Other expenses	$ _____
Total Variable Expense	$ _____

TOTAL MONTHLY EXPENSE

Monthly Income	$ _____
Less: Monthly expenses	$ _____

TOTAL NET MONTHLY INCOME BEFORE TAXES $ _____

ANNUAL BUDGET

FIXED ANNUAL EXPENSES

Mortgages	$ _____	
Loans	$ _____	
Rents	$ _____	
Insurance	$ _____	
Estimated Taxes	$ _____	
Total Fixed Monthly Expenses		$ _____

VARIABLE (controllable) ANNUAL EXPENSES

Telephone	$ _____	
Gas & electricity	$ _____	
Accounts payable	$ _____	
Travel & entertainment	$ _____	
Vehicle fuel & maintenance	$ _____	
Laundry & cleaning	$ _____	
Dues & subscriptions	$ _____	
Wages	$ _____	
Payroll taxes	$ _____	
Commissions	$ _____	
Office supplies	$ _____	
Postage	$ _____	
Other expenses	$ _____	
Total Variable Expense		$ _____

TOTAL ANNUAL EXPENSES

Annual Income	$ _____	
Less: Annual expenses	$ _____	

TOTAL NET ANNUAL INCOME BEFORE TAXES $ _____

BREAK-EVEN ANALYSIS

	Fixed Costs	Controllable Costs
Product costs		
Average cost of product	$ _____	$ _____
Monthly selling expenses		
Sales salaries and commissions	$ _____	$ _____
Advertising	$ _____	$ _____
Miscellaneous selling expense	$ _____	$ _____
Monthly general expense		
Office salaries	$ _____	$ _____
Supplies	$ _____	$ _____
Miscellaneous general expense	$ _____	$ _____
Totals	$ _____	$ _____

Number of units produced _____

Average selling price per unit $ _____

Results

Contribution margin per unit $ _____

Monthly unit sales at break-even point _____

Monthly sales dollars at break-even point $ _____

INCOME STATEMENT

Pro forma for the _____ months ending _____

INCOME
Gross sales $ _____
Less: Returns and allowances   _____
Net Sales $ _____

COST OF GOODS SOLD
Inventory beginning _____ $ _____
Production Material & Supplies   _____
Production wages   _____
Subtotal $ _____
Less: Inventory ending _____   _____
Total cost of goods sold $ _____

Gross Profit $ _____

OPERATING EXPENSES
Wages $ _____
Commissions   _____
Advertising   _____
Depreciation and amortization   _____
Employee benefits   _____
Payroll taxes   _____
Insurance   _____
Rent   _____
Utilities   _____
Office supplies   _____
Travel and entertainment   _____
Postage   _____
Interest   _____
Furniture and small equipment   _____
Other expenses   _____

_____   _____
_____   _____

Total operating expense $ _____

NET PROFIT BEFORE TAXES $ _____

TAXES PAID OR ESTIMATED TO BE PAID $ _____

NET INCOME (LOSS) $ _____

INCOME STATEMENT

For the years of _____, _____, & _____

INCOME
Gross sales $ _____ $_____ $_____
     Less: Returns and allowances _____ _____ _____
     Net Sales $ _____ $_____ $_____

COST OF GOODS SOLD
Inventory beginning _____ $ _____ $_____ $_____
Production Material & Supplies
Production wages
     Subtotal $ _____ $_____ $_____
Less: Inventory ending _____
     Total cost of goods sold $ _____ $_____ $_____

Gross Profit
     $ _____ $_____ $_____

OPERATING EXPENSES
Wages $ _____ $_____ $_____
Commissions
Advertising
Depreciation and amortization
Employee benefits
Payroll taxes
Taxes other than payroll
Insurance
Rent
Utilities
Office supplies
Travel and entertainment
Postage
Interest
Furniture and small equipment
Other expenses

_____

_____

     Total operating expense $ _____ $_____ $_____

NET PROFIT BEFORE TAXES
     $ _____ $_____ $_____

TAXES PAID OR ESTIMATED TO BE PAID $ _____ $_____ $_____

NET INCOME (LOSS)
     $ _____ $_____ $_____

CASH FLOW ANALYSIS
For the year _____

	Jan.	Feb.	Mar.	Apr.	May	June
Opening cash balance	$ _____	$ _____	$ _____	$ _____	$ _____	$ _____
Cash from operations	_____	_____	_____	_____	_____	_____
Total available cash	_____	_____	_____	_____	_____	_____
Less:						
Capital expenditures	_____	_____	_____	_____	_____	_____
Operating expenses (from Income Statement)	_____	_____	_____	_____	_____	_____
Interest	_____	_____	_____	_____	_____	_____
Dividends	_____	_____	_____	_____	_____	_____
Debt retirement	_____	_____	_____	_____	_____	_____
Other	_____	_____	_____	_____	_____	_____
Total disbursements	$ _____	$ _____	$ _____	$ _____	$ _____	$ _____
Cash Surplus (Deficit)	$ _____	$ _____	$ _____	$ _____	$ _____	$ _____
Add:						
Short-term loans	_____	_____	_____	_____	_____	_____
Long-term loans	_____	_____	_____	_____	_____	_____
Capital stock issues	_____	_____	_____	_____	_____	_____
Total additions	$ _____	$ _____	$ _____	$ _____	$ _____	$ _____
Closing cash balance	$ _____	$ _____	$ _____	$ _____	$ _____	$ _____

	July	Aug.	Sept.	Oct.	Nov.	Dec.
Opening cash balance	$ _____	$ _____	$ _____	$ _____	$ _____	$ _____
Cash from operations	_____	_____	_____	_____	_____	_____
Total available cash	_____	_____	_____	_____	_____	_____
Less:						
Capital expenditures	_____	_____	_____	_____	_____	_____
Operating expenses (from Income Statement)	_____	_____	_____	_____	_____	_____
Interest	_____	_____	_____	_____	_____	_____
Dividends	_____	_____	_____	_____	_____	_____
Debt retirement	_____	_____	_____	_____	_____	_____
Other	_____	_____	_____	_____	_____	_____
Total disbursements	$ _____	$ _____	$ _____	$ _____	$ _____	$ _____
Cash Surplus (Deficit)	$ _____	$ _____	$ _____	$ _____	$ _____	$ _____
Add:						
Short-term loans	_____	_____	_____	_____	_____	_____
Long-term loans	_____	_____	_____	_____	_____	_____
Capital stock issues	_____	_____	_____	_____	_____	_____
Total additions	$ _____	$ _____	$ _____	$ _____	$ _____	$ _____
Closing cash balance	$ _____	$ _____	$ _____	$ _____	$ _____	$ _____

CASH FLOW ANALYSIS

For the years _____, _____, & _____

Opening cash balance	$	$	$
Cash from operations			
Total available cash			
Less:			
Capital expenditures			
Operating expenses (from Income Statement)			
Interest			
Dividends			
Debt retirement			
Other			
Total disbursements	$	$	$
Cash Surplus (deficit)	$	$	$
Add:			
Short-term loans			
Long-term loans			
Capital stock issues			
Total additions	$	$	$
Closing cash balance	$	$	$

MARKETING PLAN

This is the marketing plan of _____

I. MARKET ANALYSIS

A. Target Market - Who are the customers?

1. We will be selling primarily to (check all that apply):

	Total Percent	of Business
a. Private sector	_____	_____
b. Wholesalers	_____	_____
c. Retailers	_____	_____
d. Government	_____	_____
e. Other	_____	_____

2. We will be targeting customers by:

a. Product line/services.
   We will target specific lines   _____
b. Geographic area? Which areas? _____
c. Sales? We will target sales of   _____
d. Industry? Our target industry is   _____
e. Other?   _____

3. How much will our selected market spend on our type of product or service this coming year?

$_____

B. Competition

1. Who are our competitors?

NAME   _____
ADDRESS   _____
_____

Years in Business _____

Market Share _____
Price/Strategy _____
Product/Service Features_____

NAME _____
ADDRESS _____
_____

Years in Business _____
Market Share _____
Price/Strategy _____
Product/Service Features_____

2. How competitive is the market?

High _____
Medium _____
Low _____

3. List below your strengths and weaknesses compared to your competition (consider such areas as location, size of resources, reputation, services, personnel, etc.):

Strengths	Weaknesses
1. _____	1. _____
2. _____	2. _____
3. _____	3. _____
4. _____	4. _____

C. Environment

1. The following are some important economic factors that will affect our product or service (such as trade area growth, industry health, economic trends, taxes, rising energy prices, etc.):

_____
_____
_____

2. The following are some important legal factors that
   will affect our market:

   _____

   _____

   _____

3. The following are some important government factors:

   _____

   _____

   _____

4. The following are other environmental factors that will affect our market, but
   over which we have no control:

   _____

   _____

   _____

II. PRODUCT OR SERVICE ANALYSIS

A. Description

1. Describe here what the product/service is and what it does:

   _____

   _____

   _____

   _____

B. Comparison

1. What advantages does our product/service have over those of the
   competition (consider such things as unique features, patents, expertise,
   special training, etc.)?

   _____

   _____

   _____

   _____

2. What disadvantages does it have?

   _____

   _____

   _____

   _____

C. Other Factors

    1. Where will you get your materials and supplies?

_____

_____

    2. List other considerations:

_____

_____

_____

_____

III. MARKETING STRATEGIES - MARKET MIX

A. Image

What kind of image do we want to have (such as cheap but good, or exclusiveness, or customer-oriented or highest quality, or convenience, or speed, or other)?

_____

B. Features

List the features we will emphasize:

    a. _____

    b. _____

    c. _____

C. Pricing

    1. We will be using the following pricing strategy:

        a. Markup on cost   _____   What % markup? _____

        b. Suggested price   _____

        c. Competitive   _____

        d. Below competition _____

        e. Premium price   _____

        f. Other   _____

    2. Are our prices in line with our image?

        YES_____   NO _____

    3. Do our prices cover costs and leave a margin of profit?

        YES_____   NO _____

D. Customer Services

    1. List the customer services we provide:

        a. _____

        b. _____

        c. _____

    2. These are our sales/credit terms:

        a. _____

        b. _____

        c. _____

    3. The competition offers the following services:

        a. _____

        b. _____

        c. _____

E. Advertising/Promotion

    1. These are the things we wish to say about the business:

        _____

        _____

        _____

    2. We will use the following advertising/promotion sources:

        1. Television   _____

        2. Radio   _____

        3. Direct mail   _____

        4. Personal contacts   _____

        5. Trade associations   _____

        6. Newspaper   _____

        7. Magazines   _____

        8. Yellow Pages   _____

        9. Billboard   _____

        10. Other _____   _____

    3. The following are the reasons why we consider the media we have chosen to be the most effective:

        _____

        _____

OTHER INFORMATION

INSURANCE

Company _____ Policy # _____

Coverage _____ Premium _____

LOANS/OUTSTANDING DEBTS

Lender _____

Original Amount_____ Balance Unpaid _____

COMPETITIVE PROJECTIONS

Other resources needed to become competitive: _____

_____

_____

Years projected to become competitive: _____

LICENSES/PERMITS/CERTIFICATES

Type	Amount	Issuer
_____	_____	_____
_____	_____	_____
_____	_____	_____
_____	_____	_____
_____	_____	_____

Intellectual Property: _____

_____

_____

_____

_____

_____

_____

_____

MISCELLANEOUS

Trade associations/organizations of membership: _____

_____

_____

_____

_____

Contracts with suppliers: _____

_____

_____

_____

Liens, judgments, or lawsuits in force or pending: _____

_____

_____

_____

_____

Glossary of useful terms

A-B

Accounting Period

A specific period of time used for record keeping and reporting.

Articles of Incorporation

The terms under which a business incorporates, generally stating the who, where, when, why and how of the corporation.

Assets

Items of value to a business.

Balance Sheet

A schedule of assets, liabilities and capital (net worth).

Board of Directors

Persons who have been chosen or elected to govern the operation of a corporation.

Break-even point

The point where the income from a company's business equals expenses, and realizes neither a profit nor loss.

Budget

A plan for detailing how money will be spent over a specific time period.

Capital

Income or value place on an item or amount.

Cost of goods sold

The cost incurred in the production of products or materials held for sale.

Creditor

A person or company which is owed money, product or service from another person or company.

d/b/a

The name under which a company conducts business if different than its registered name.

Depreciation

The method of periodically reducing the value of an asset over its useful life. *Current depreciation* refers to the deduction for the current accounting period. *Accumulated depreciation* refers to the total amount of depreciation by which an asset has been reduced.

Fiscal Year

An accounting year which ends on any date other than December 31.

Intangible Assets

An asset which has value, but does not exist to sight or touch.

Intellectual Assets

Royalties, royalty arrangements, copyrights, patents, exclusive use contracts and notes receivable from officers and employees.

Goodwill

The intangible value placed on a product or service.

Gross Profit

The amount of profit shown on the book of record after Cost of goods sold and returns and allowances have been deducted.

Leasehold Improvements

Permanent improvements which have been made to any property which is leased.

Liability

An amount which is owed to another, this could include products or services.

Long-term Asset

A capital asset having a life expectancy of greater than one year.

Mission Statement

The official statement of a business regarding what type of business it is and what the business is planning to accomplish.

Operating Expenses

Expenses of the business which do not relate to the production and sales of materials, but rather to the actual cost of operating the business.

Pro forma

Any statement which is a projection or representation of future expectations.

Recapture Value

The anticipated salvage value remaining after an asset has passed its useful life expectancy or become unrepairable, and is not subject to depreciation.

Retained Earnings

Funds which have not as yet been distributed or applied.

Short-term Assets

Assets which have an anticipated life span of one year or less. Also known as Liquid (or quick) assets.

Start-up Capital

A schedule which lists where and how much money will be spent to get the business to a point where it can sustain itself.

Tangible Asset

A "real" asset which may be touched or seen, such as a machine.

Whatever you need to know, we've made it E-Z!

Informative text and forms you can fill out on-screen.* From personal to business, legal to leisure—we've made it E-Z!

PERSONAL & FAMILY

For all your family's needs, we have titles that will help keep you organized and guide you through most every aspect of your personal life.

BUSINESS

Whether you're starting from scratch with a home business or you just want to keep your corporate records in shape, we've got the programs for you.

* Not all topics include forms   ss 1999.r2

By the book...

	Item#	Qty.	Price Ea.‡
Made E•Z Software			
ccounting Made E-Z	SW1207		$29.95
sset Protection Made E-Z	SW1157		$29.95
ankruptcy Made E-Z	SW1154		$29.95
usiness Startups Made E-Z	SW1192		$29.95
uying/Selling Your Home Made E-Z	SW1213		$29.95
ar Buying Made E-Z	SW1146		$29.95
orporate Record Keeping Made E-Z	SW1159		$29.95
redit Repair Made E-Z	SW1153		$29.95
ivorce Law Made E-Z	SW1182		$29.95
veryday Law Made E-Z	SW1185		$29.95
veryday Legal Forms & Agreements	SW1186		$29.95
corporation Made E-Z	SW1176		$29.95
ast Wills Made E-Z	SW1177		$29.95
ving Trusts Made E-Z	SW1178		$29.95
ffshore Investing Made E-Z	SW1218		$29.95
wning a Franchise Made E-Z	SW1202		$29.95
our Profitable Home Business	SW1204		$29.95
Made E•Z Guides			
ankruptcy Made E-Z	G200		$17.95
corporation Made E-Z	G201		$17.95
ivorce Law Made E-Z	G202		$17.95
redit Repair Made E-Z	G203		$17.95
ving Trusts Made E-Z	G205		$17.95
ving Wills Made E-Z	G206		$17.95
ast Wills Made E-Z	G207		$17.95
mall Claims Court Made E-Z	G209		$17.95
affic Court Made E-Z	G210		$17.95
uying/Selling Your Home Made E-Z	G211		$17.95
mployment Law Made E-Z	G212		$17.95
nmigration Made E-Z	G213		$17.95
ollecting Child Support Made E-Z	G215		$17.95
mited Liability Companies Made E-Z	G216		$17.95
artnerships Made E-Z	G218		$17.95
olving IRS Problems Made E-Z	G219		$17.95
sset Protection Made E-Z	G220		$17.95
uying/Selling A Business Made E-Z	G221		$17.95
aising Venture Capital Made E-Z	G222		$17.95
rofitable Mail Order Made E-Z	G223		$17.95
-Commerce Made E-Z	G224		$17.95
3A Loans Made E-Z	G225		$17.95
oubleshooting Your Business Made E-Z	G226		$17.95
dvertising & Promoting Your Business	G227		$17.95
apid Reading Made E-Z	G228		$17.95
veryday Math Made E-Z	G229		$17.95
noestring Investing Made E-Z	G230		$17.95
ock Market Investing Made E-Z	G231		$17.95
ndraising Made E-Z	G232		$17.95
op Smoking Made E-Z	G233		$17.95
ollege Funding Made E-Z	G234		$17.95
arketing Your Small Business	G235		$17.95
wning A No-Cash-Down Business	G236		$17.95
ffshore Investing Made E-Z	G237		$17.95
-L-M Made E-Z	G238		$17.95
ee Legal Help Made E-Z	G239		$17.95
ee Stuff For Everyone Made E-Z	G240		$17.95
ur Profitable Home Business Made E-Z	G241		$17.95
siness Plans Made E-Z	G242		$17.95
utual Fund Investing Made E-Z	G243		$17.95
Made E•Z Books			
anaging Employees Made E-Z	BK308		$29.95
orporate Record Keeping Made E-Z	BK310		$29.95
tal Record Keeping Made E-Z	BK312		$29.95
usiness Forms Made E-Z	BK313		$29.95
ollecting Unpaid Bills Made E-Z	BK309		$29.95
veryday Law Made E-Z	BK311		$29.95
veryday Legal Forms & Agreements	BK307		$29.95
SHIPPING & HANDLING *			$
orida Residents add 6% sales tax			$
TOTAL OF ORDER			$

Index

A-O •••••

P-Y•••••